# A Bib

by Barbra Bateson
illustrated by Margeaux Lewis

Practice Decodable 16

McGraw Hill Education

Bothell, WA • Chicago, IL • Columbus, OH • New York, NY

MHEonline.com



Send all inquiries to:
McGraw-Hill Education
8787 Orion Place
Columbus, OH 43240

ISBN: 978-0-02-132675-4
MHID: 0-02-132675-4

Printed in the United States of America.

7 8 9 CTM 23

Bob had a bib.

Plop! Mom blots at a spot.

Plop! Dad blots at a spot.

Mom and Dad had bad spots.

Did a bib have a spot?

The bib on Bob did not!